The Lord's Prayer

www.iCharacter.org

Published by iCharacter Limited ®. (Ireland)
By Agnes de Bezenac
Illustrated by Agnes de Bezenac
Colored by Henny Y.
All Bible verses adapted from the KJV.

Copyright © 2020 by iCharacter Limited ®. All rights reserved. No part of this book may be reproduced in any form or by any electronic or mechanical means, including information storage and retrieval systems, without written permission from the publisher or author, except in the case of a reviewer, who may quote brief passages embodied in critical articles or in a review.

Dear Daddy in heaven.
I love you and I want to get to know you better.

Please make things right, here on earth, just like you do in heaven.

You always know what's best.

Thank you
for taking such good care of me.

Please give me what I need today, and help me to be content with it.

Forgive me when I hurt others. And help me to forgive those that hurt me.

I want to learn to do what is right.

Be kind

My God,
my King, you are strong and you are powerful.

Thank you for always loving me, without ever stopping.

MY Shepherd

I am content

I'm a little sheep, a very happy sheep.
I have everything that I need.

I take a big bite of grass. Munch, munch!
Juicy and crunchy, my favorite.

And over there is a stream of water.
Sip. Sip. Cool and fresh, just perfect.

Such peace

I lay on the soft grass. It's so quiet and calm here. Look at the sky! Wow! I can see fluffy puffy clouds making fun shapes. There's the sun to keep me warm, and there's my good shepherd.

He loves me and makes me smile.

Not afraid

"It's time to go home, little sheep!"
my shepherd calls.

Oh my, it's dark now... I'm afraid.
"Don't be afraid," my shepherd says.
He stands close beside me. He points
with his shepherd's staff to lead the way.

"Growl!" What's that I hear?
Quick as a flash, my strong shepherd
defends me from danger.

Bubbling with joy

He takes me home. At last, I am safe and secure. My legs jump and wiggle. That's what I do when I'm content. And if I'm really really happy, I sing. I'm full of joy and it all wants to come out.

Always there

My shepherd is always with me. From the time I was born till the rest of my life. For always!

Thank you Jesus for being my good shepherd. With you I am safe. With you I am happy. I am blessed.

More from iCharacter.org

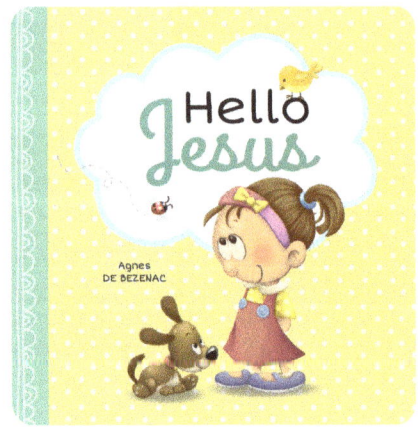
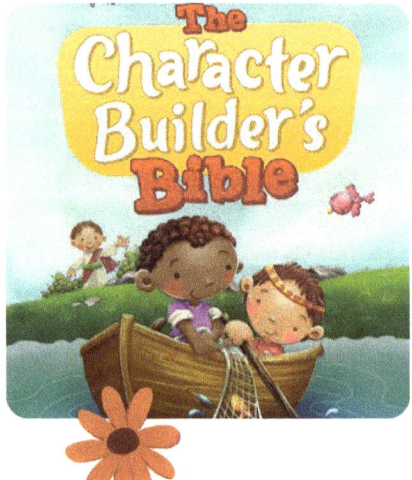

www.ingramcontent.com/pod-product-compliance
Lightning Source LLC
Chambersburg PA
CBHW040013080526
44586CB00028B/2994